Quotable General

QUOTABLE
GENERAL

WORDS OF WISDOM, MOTIVATION, AND SUCCESS BY AND ABOUT BOBBY KNIGHT, BASKETBALL'S UNRIVALED TEACHER

Monte Carpenter

TowleHouse Publishing
Nashville, Tennessee

TowleHouse books are distributed by National Book Network
(NBN), 4720 Boston Way, Lanham, Maryland 20706.

Cataloging-in-Publication data is available.
ISBN: 1-931249-02-4

Cover design by Gore Studio, Inc.
Page design by Mike Towle

Printed in the United States of America
1 2 3 4 5 6 — 05 04 03 02 01

TABLE OF CONTENTS

ACKNOWLEDGMENTS

Researching and compiling a work of this nature is possible only through the willing assistance of a number of people. My thanks go to the following people who shouldered much of that burden:

Jeff Fanter, Kim Dunning, and the University of Indiana basketball media relations office staff were gracious in allowing me to spend the better part of two days combing through reams of file material;

Bradley Cook, reference specialist and photograph curator for the Indiana University Archives, was accommodating and patient for hours on end while I pored through stacks of material;

Bob Hammel, veteran Bloomington, Indiana, scribe and friend to Coach Knight, pointed me in the right direction at crucial times when I wasn't sure where to turn;

Photographer Paul Riley helped me get to the finish line in one piece;

Brian Hogaboom of the Army Athletic Association at the United States Military Academy went the extra mile in chasing down some resources;

Tesa Riddle was her usual thorough self in reviewing the manuscript;

My wife, Holley, and son, Andrew, allowed me the freedom to go out of town for days on end or to sequester myself in my office for hours at a time in pulling this project together;

Finally, to our Lord, Jesus Christ, for being the safety net who makes all trials and tribulations bearable.

INTRODUCTION

College basketball missed Coach Bobby Knight as soon as the 2000–2001 season got underway. Indiana University fans missed their idolized general, once voted "the Most Influential Coach in America" by his coaching peers. Members of the media missed him because Knight made good press, whether it involved his disdain for clichés or his occasionally controversial nature, at times confrontational. Purists of the game missed Knight for his expert and disciplined demonstration of how the game should be played. Dick Vitale missed him. So did Billy Packer. So did a whole bunch of others.

In September 2000, Indiana University president Myles Brand abruptly fired Knight, abruptly ending his twenty-nine-year stint as the school's men's basketball coach. Knight's Hoosiers teams had won three NCAA Tournament titles and 73.4 percent of their games overall while averaging twenty-three victories a season. Including his six seasons as head coach at West Point, Knight left Indiana with 763 career victories, leaving him seventh on college basketball's all-time victory list that is topped by Dean Smith (879 victories) and Adolph Rupp (876). Knight's 1975–76 national championship team finished 32-0, a perfect final record which, going into the 2000—2001 season, still had not been matched by any other Division I school. Knight, the winningest coach in Big Ten history, was the youngest head coach to get to 200 career victories. Ditto for 300, 400, 500, 600, and 700.

Here is a Knight triple crown that has been matched by only
one other man: (1) an NCAA Championship as a player (1960
with Ohio State), (2) an NCAA title as a coach (1976, 1981, and
1987 with Indiana), and (3) an Olympic gold medal as a coach
(1984)—all accomplished during a career that never crossed paths
with the pros (not yet anyway). The other man—Dean Smith.

In light of all the critical media attention Knight received in
2000—most of it somehow relating to either Pepperdine, Neil Reed,
zero tolerance, Kent Harvey, or Myles Brand—he finished the year
(and the twentieth century) bombarded with characterizations that
didn't paint a pretty picture: bully, intimidator, raging tyrant, uncon-
trolled angryman. Knight was an easy target, haunted by his past.
Critics used the opportunity as carte blanche to dredge up and, in
some cases, embellish Knight's past temper-related antics to make a
case that it was time for IU administrators to lock the door on
Knight and throw away the key. Some of the recalled incidents mer-
ited a revisit, some didn't. An example of the latter was renewed
(and revised) accounts of Knight's confrontation with a Puerto
Rican security guard at the 1979 Pan-American Games—when
Knight was provoked, and poked in the eye, by a small-time cop on
a big-time power trip. Only now, more than twenty years later, we
are to believe that Knight brazenly *assaulted* the upstanding cop that
day as if the guy were just another LSU fan headed for the trash can,
and therefore Knight should be fired, for life.

Take away the incidents and the innuendo, and we are left
with a glass half full that puts Knight into an all-time elite class of
college basketball coaches that includes the likes of Clair Bee, Hank
Iba, Pete Newell, John Wooden, Mike Krzyzewski, Rupp, and Smith.
Knight was, and is, a great coach, although he prefers the term

teacher. Knight has long brandished the teacher tag not only as a counterpunch to university professors who had long called for his dismissal at IU, but also because the gymnasium was his classroom. Distractions of any sort were not tolerated, and players—his students—were often required to take written notes. It obviously had a carryover effect. Note: All but two of his eighty or so four-year players at Indiana earned their degrees. Through all this, nary an NCAA sanction for rules violations. Knight insisted on playing, and winning, by the rules. He is intensely loyal to players loyal to him, and he probably understands the game's intricacies and its ebb and flow more than any other man alive.

Knight does not suffer fools, nor does he tolerate slackers, meddlesome alumni, lazy game officials, rebels, or inquiring media minds whose unspoken intent is to elicit anger instead of an answer from the coach. Much of the public doesn't realize it, but many Knight press conferences usually include a sprinkling of inexplicably credentialed "reporters" whose sole annoying purpose is to ask inane or inflammatory questions just to get under the coach's skin and manufacture an outburst that then gets played up as a news event. Understand that Knight is a target wherever he goes.

Knight is honest to a fault, if that's possible, and he does not embrace political correctness—this in a country where dishonesty and political correctness are acceptable means to an end. Knight admits it: He is an anachronism. Still, reporters who cover college basketball miss Knight—even those who were quick to write disparagingly about him. Reporters are paid to generate good copy and Knight is full of angles, wittingly (and wittily) or unwittingly.

Often overlooked in the Knight hype is his refreshing candor and analytical insights on a variety of subjects. He has a good sense of humor that often crosses over into sarcasm, and his amazing recall is evident when asked about specific teams and games from years long past. He not only can dissect the game's X's and O's with incredible clarity, he can successfully and succinctly communicate those details to willing listeners. Knight, once the student, now forever the teacher, is remembered in *Quotable General* as a man who had a lot to say over the years. He never backed down from an issue, touchy or otherwise. This compilation of quotes by and about Knight reveals as much about the man's motivations as it does the extent of his wisdom.

THE ARMY WAY

"They march to lunch: they march to dinner. Chin in: Chest out. Gut in. All day."

—BOB KNIGHT

On being only twenty-four years old when he became the head basketball coach at Army:
My age never really concerned me. I didn't know a hell of a lot about basketball, but I knew how I thought the game should be played, and I knew that I could coach it the way I thought it should be played.[1]

~

We had an excellent preseason conditioning program at West Point. It was set up by the captain of the team, and the players were coming in on their own time after classes.[2]

~

To get the results I wanted (at West Point), I was certain I had to be just as tough as the very toughest tactical officer there. So I had to conduct a program even more demanding.[3]

~

Our talent was such that a single bad call could beat us, so I wasn't about to let two guys with whistles take away what we had worked so hard to achieve.[4]

~

WHEN YOU TELL THEM ABOUT ME, MAKE SURE YOU TELL THEM I DID-N'T HAVE ANYTHING TO DO WITH THE SCREAMING AND ALL THAT.[5]
—*Fred Taylor, Knight's coach at Ohio State and one of Knight's mentors*

⌒

At West Point I made up my mind to win—gotta win. Not at all costs. Never that. But winning was the hub of everything I was doing. And understand, I've never gotten over West Point. Winning had to be more important there, and I had a point to prove. I was just coming off a playing career during which I didn't do as well as I'd hoped.[6]

⌒

People take Patton—a tough, demanding individualist—and equate him with me. Well, that's not what I try to imitate. He sacrificed people. My basic idea is, Let's live and fight tomorrow.[7]

⌒

I have never met Colonel (Red) Blaik at West Point, but I tried to study everything that had made him a winner in that environment. I talked to his former players; I went over his every move. And then I patterned myself after him. Colonel Blaik was an extremely intelligent individual and he was a great organizer. The ability to prepare to win is just as important as the will.[8]

It is a fallacy to say that Army's players are naturally disciplined. They are up at ten minutes before six because they have to be. They are required to go to class. They march to lunch: they march to dinner. Chin in: Chest out. Gut in. All day. Well, when four o'clock comes and it's time to practice basketball, the most natural thing for them to do is to expect to relax and have fun.[9]

The whole idea of what West Point stood for had a special interest to me, and as I stayed there, my feelings about it became stronger and stronger. West Point is an absolutely outstanding institutional concept.[10]

A young Knight was a good fit for the cadets of West Point, and vice versa. (United States Military Academy photo)

Patton had an incredible ability to see what he had to do and how to do it. But I think he was pompous beyond what his position called for. MacArthur was also an incredibly arrogant, pompous guy. Yet he engaged more enemy troops with fewer casualties than any other military commander in history. That, to me, is the mark of a great general. But I think my choice as the greatest military commander of all is Ulysses S. Grant . . . Grant wore the uniform of a private. He had no self-interest at all. He never tried to promote himself in any way. He felt he was a soldier given a job to do, a distasteful job, and that was to get the war over as quickly as he could. That was his only objective.[11]

HE'S A COACH THAT RESPECTS YOUR GAME AND YOU AS A PERSON. I WOULDN'T CALL HIM A FRIEND, THOUGH. HE'S MORE OF A DRILL SERGEANT. BUT A FRIENDLY SERGEANT.[12]

—*Greg Graham, IU player, 1989–93*

INDIANA WANTS ME

"I couldn't have picked anyplace as well-suited for me as Indiana."

—BOB KNIGHT

I THOUGHT FROM THE VERY BEGINNING THAT BOB KNIGHT SHOULD COACH HERE. THE MAN HAS A THOROUGHNESS OF MIND THAT SETS HIM APART FROM THE MANY APPLICANTS WE REVIEWED. IT WASN'T SO MUCH HIS COACHING RECORD AS THE QUALITY OF THE MAN THAT LED TO THE CHOICE. FOR HIS AGE, THERE ISN'T A MAN IN THE COUNTRY WHO HAS ACCOMPLISHED AS MUCH.[1]

> —*Dr. Edwin Cady, Indiana University's Big Ten representative and screening committee member after Knight was hired in March 1971 to coach the Hoosiers*

ACCORDING TO ATHLETIC DIRECTOR BILL ORWIG, THE SCREENING COMMITTEE INTERVIEWING CANDIDATES FOR IU'S BASKETBALL HEAD-COACHING JOB IN 1971 WAS UNANIMOUS IN PICKING KNIGHT AFTER EVALUATING EACH CANDIDATE ON THE BASIS OF THE FOLLOWING FIVE QUESTIONS:

- WHICH WOULD BEST EXEMPLIFY WHAT INDIANA WANTS?
- CAN HE TEACH AND EDUCATE?
- WILL HE GET US IN TROUBLE?
- DOES HE CONVEY THE IMAGE THE UNIVERSITY WANTS?
- WILL HE "WEAR" WELL?[2]

OUR COACH FOR INFINITY.

*—IU athletic director Bill Orwig, introducing Knight
in March 1971 as the school's new coach*

I couldn't have picked anyplace as well-suited for me as
Indiana.

I'll bet that if we had had basketball in the early 1800s, Abe
Lincoln would just naturally have stayed in Indiana rather
than go on to Illinois. Some coach would have recognized his
potential to become a great rebounder. He undoubtedly
would have become a coach and won several state championships instead of spending a lot of time talking with some
fellow named Douglas.[3]

I told my wife (Nancy) I'll see her when we get the players.[4]
—Knight, *after taking the IU job, referring to heading out on the recruiting trail*

An Indiana player is one who can only be defeated by a clock that happens to run out of time. He is what every boy wants to become and what an old man can look back upon with great pride that he once was.[5]

An Indiana basketball player can come in any size, shape, or color. There is no common ground except a love for the game and a desire to get the most out of his abilities.[6]

When we bring in a kid for a visit, we always have our players go out with him. If they turn him down, that's it. We don't recruit him.[7]

When we're recruiting, I tell the parents I expect certain things from kids . . . I tell them that playing for me will be more demanding than anyplace else they can go and that I believe that if they entrust their son with me, that I have the responsibility to see that he grows as much toward his potential as he possibly can.[8]

Knight was a quick study at Indiana. (Indiana University Archives)

HE WAS THE FIRST GUY WHO DIDN'T B.S. WHEN HE RECRUITED ME.[9]
—*Scott May, IU great who was college basketball's 1975–76 Player of the Year*

College entrance requirements for athletes today are at an absolute minimum. If a kid can't handle these requirements, he doesn't belong in college.[10]

An Indiana player has the enthusiasm of an evangelist, the discipline of a monk, and the heart of a warrior (who) never loses the honesty and character of a small boy.

We've drawn up a personality profile, and you might even say it's a narrow-minded thing.[11]

I try to get a kid who I think can play the way I want him to play. I want a kid who can adjust to the roles we establish for him. I want a kid who is not going to be an academic derelict.

I've found out it's really important to talk to mothers. I try to visit on the night when the old man's not home. All he's going to ask is how many shots Johnny is going to get . . . Mothers say, "What's Johnny going to eat?"

⌐⌐

Recruiting junior college kids is an interesting thing. I've had a phobia about them for a long time. Either they were there because they weren't good students or they were a pain in the butt, whatever.[12]

—*About refusing to recruit JUCO players until 1983*

⌐⌐

The reason I put that banner up in 1983 is because of how great the fans were. You are a very big part of Indiana basketball. You make it enjoyable when I hear you react to something good that we do out here.[13]

—*Knight speaking at an open forum at Assembly Hall, explaining why IU's 1983 Big Ten title banner was the only banner hung in Assembly Hall for a Knight team*

⌐⌐

WE'RE KNIGHT GOING TO TAKE IT ANYMORE.
> —*placard at a rally on Knight's behalf in April 2000*

Those "All You Can Be" commercials may be sophisticated for people at Purdue, but our kids down here are a little too smart for those things.
> —*speaking to IU student body in November 1991 before introducing wounded Gulf War soldier Darren Murphy, a Purdue student*

The 1975 team was the best one, even thought they didn't win the championship. Great defense and the best offense.
> —*Knight in a 1989 television interview with Bob Costas*

Hey! If this is the best our crowd can do getting after us, then there's something missing. We'd rather be playing in front of no one.[14]
> —*Knight grabbing the P.A. microphone during an IU game against Northwestern, with the Hoosiers up by twelve points*

THE LORD IS OUR SHEPHERD AND BOB KNIGHT IS OUR COACH.

> *—Sign held by fans rallying to Knight's defense after*
> *the Neil Reed story broke in March 2000*

SEND NEIL REED TO CUBA AND KEEP ELIAN.

> *—Another sign held by fans rallying to Knight's defense*

INDIANA BASKETBALL IS SOMETHING SPECIAL. IT'S SOMETHING THAT YOU DREAM OF, BEING ABLE TO COME HERE AND PLAY FOR COACH KNIGHT.[15]

> *—Damon Bailey, Indiana high school legend*
> *and former Hoosier guard under Knight*

Let's get serious! (Indiana University Archives)

One thing I have always taken pride in, with the student body, is how hard the students had rooted for us.[16]

Let him be a student. And let him get on with his life. This thing had happened to me long before that situation took place. That kid is not responsible for my not coaching at Indiana.

> —Knight referring to Kent Harvey, the IU student whose disrespectful greeting of Knight led to events that culminated in Knight's dismissal from Indiana

COACH AND
TEACHER

*"I would rather be thought of
as a teacher than a coach."*

—BOB KNIGHT

I teach out there on the floor for three hours every day, and I look upon this as the same kind of classroom that a history professor has or a chemistry professor has.[1]

A coach must remember that he is a teacher and therefore must prepare his team for every possible situation that may develop.[2]

Everyone remembers more when we write things down.[3]

What has been emphasized generally can be discussed specifically.[4]

The basketball classroom is one of the most demanding there is. Not only are there principles to be learned, but there's an immediate practical application of those theories.[5]

One of the essentials in teaching is to emphasize. How do you emphasize? Quietly? On occasion. By not saying anything? I think you can. By really making a vocally emphatic point? Sure. You have to be a lot of different things.[6]

The best teachers I've known are intolerant people. They don't tolerate mistakes.[7]

I think every coach is ready to quit at some point every year.[8]

If you haven't coached, one of the most difficult things to understand is a coach's mentality. For everybody else . . . it is entertainment. If we get beat, our fans take it hard, but they get over it quickly. But coaches don't. When things aren't going well, it can be a very difficult profession.[9]

There's probably nobody that's ever coached basketball that just likes the game any better than I do. I mean I really like the game.[10]

Hoosier teammates Scott May and Quinn Buckner, leaders of the 1974–75 and 1975–76 teams that won sixty-three of sixty-four games, go over some X's and O's with Coach Knight. (Indiana University Archives)

It's not as good a game for a coach today as it once was. The three-point shot and the thirty-five-second clock take away from coaching. You don't have to be quite as good a coach, with those two things, as you once had to do.[11]

Coaching is a great balance between demand and patience. The coaches who are demanding—constantly demanding— are not particularly good coaches. The coaches who are extremely patient are not particularly good coaches. There's a balance between the two that I think is really important. Patience allows for development; demand brings about development at a rate that you have to have.[12]

There are a lot of things that really amuse me, and one is, professors have occasionally, in either groups or, I'm not ever sure individually, but in the security of groups, taken me on in one way or another, and among them have been professors that couldn't teach lions to get red meat. And that amuses me, because I've taught my students pretty well.[13]

I teach. I think of myself as a teacher. I'm not a recruiter and, as the press has constantly reminded me, I'm not a P.R. expert. Our practice is set up as a two-hour class. If one of my players ever says he learned more from playing basketball than anything else he did at Indiana University, then we've been successful.[14]

Look, the easiest way to coach is to pat everybody on the (behind). "That's okay, Johnny—you've missed nineteen shots in a row, don't hesitate." But the coach that really coaches and really teaches is the guy who goes out on a limb even though some kid isn't going to like him, or the team isn't going to like him, but he's out there doing that because it's the best way to get kids to play as well as they can.[15]

In basketball I might have been, maybe at best, an average athlete in basketball during the time I played. Baseball, I was probably a much-better-than-average athlete. But any game I've ever played, I've understood how to play.[16]

I would rather be thought of as a teacher than a coach. I've always felt that the absolute best thing that anybody could ever do for me is to tell me, "I ran into one of your players the other day and he told me that you were the best teacher he ever had."[17]

I compare the opening game of a season to birth from a coaching standpoint because I am always hoping for the best while not knowing quite what to expect.[18]

The whole idea of coaching is centered on the theme of taking a team through its various stages of growth and developing it to its full potential. Now that this year's (1977–78) team is on its way, I will use a line from the Rubaiyat of Omar Khayyam as a guide to its growth:

> "Ah, my computations, people say, have led the world to better reckoning. Nay, tis but the striking from the calendar of unborn tomorrow and dead yesterday."[19]

Society long ago decided that it has a far greater interest in the football team than it does in the chemistry program. Coaches and universities had nothing to do with it. So you are always going to have some strained relations about the position athletics holds and how people throughout the rest of the faculty feel about it.[20]

Most of my coaching is negative. I concentrate on the ways we could lose and what we can do about them.[21]

IF YOU ARE AT A PRACTICE, YOU'RE SUPPOSED TO BE TOTALLY QUIET. HE HAS UPBRAIDED PEOPLE FOR TALKING. THAT'S HIS CLASSROOM AND YOU DON'T TALK IN THE CLASSROOM; YOU LISTEN.[22]

—*Bob Hammel*

I don't think there's an official in the country who knows as much about basketball as I do. Not even close. Or as much as any other coach knows.[23]

Basketball affords me the opportunity to do the things I like to do other than basketball—and I think that's why I do it.[24]

～

Knight addressing the hypothetical of his being a classroom teacher and what kind of guidelines he would establish:
I teach one class and I tell them on the first day that if they want to wear a hat, they'd better not wear it in there. If they want to go barefoot, don't do it in my class. You don't wear shoes, you don't get in the classroom. You cut one class, it's a C. You cut two classes, it's failure.[25]

～

It's true sometimes I intimidate a kid. Usually when I first get him. That sets up the best conditions for teaching. But that's only true with basketball players, not with anyone else.[26]

～

I try to win basketball games and at the same time prepare my players for the rest of their lives.[27]

～

I have always operated under the theory that basketball is not rocket science. It doesn't take Einstein to coach basketball. If I need an inordinate amount of time to coach basketball, I must not be smart enough to figure it out in a normal amount of time.[28]

I very early realized I wasn't good enough to play after graduation (from Ohio State), so I'd better figure out something I could do.[29]

Basketball intrigues me as much as ever. Every season brings its new wrinkles—something different. Always something different. With me, it's not so much how well our players play, but how I can get them to play well. That part is getting harder and harder.[30]

LEADERSHIP

*"He continually takes players
and makes them better."*

—ISIAH THOMAS

In leadership, you're trying to get people to be better than they think they can be, to reach within themselves. You're trying to get a guy to do something he doesn't want to do—and do it well.[1]

IF YOU ARE GOING TO BE A NUMBER-ONE LEADER AND YOU WANT TO WIN, YOU ARE GOING TO HAVE TO HURT SOMEBODY'S FEELINGS AND EVERYTHING IS NOT GOING TO BE PERFECT.[2]

—*A. J. Foyt, one of Knight's friends from other sports*

YOUR DAY WILL COME, THIS I KNOW. YOUR DETERMINATION, DESIRE, AND DEVOTION TO THE GAME WILL CARRY YOU TO NEW HEIGHTS. I HOPE I AM AROUND TO CHEER FOR YOU AND YOUR TEAM WHEN THAT DAY COMES.[3]

—*Clair Bee, legendary Long Island University basketball coach, in a letter he sent to Knight after Army lost to St. John's in the semifinals of the 1970 NIT.*

I think being decisive is one of life's greatest qualities. I try to impress it on my own kids. Most people don't like to make decisions.[4]

If you don't play well, you sit on the bench. Everyone with a competitive personality, their (rear end) sends a message up to the brain, something like, "Get me the hell off of here."

⌒

HE'S VERY DEMANDING. BUT WHEN THEY GET USED TO HIM, KIDS ARE READY TO LAY DOWN THEIR LIVES FOR HIM, BECAUSE THEY WATCH HIM BLEEDING OUT HIS LIFE FOR THEM.[5]

—*Lou Carnesecca, former St. John's coach*

⌒

Obviously, I can't control every single thing that happens. That's impossible. But I do think I can set the tone. I can say, "Hey, this isn't going to happen, and I won't allow it to happen."[6]

—*Knight in a benefit speech for the Knox County Youth Shelter*

⌒

HIS METHODS OF MOTIVATING ARE MUCH MORE MENTAL THAN PHYSICAL. HE CONTINUALLY TAKES PLAYERS AND MAKES THEM BETTER. THAT'S HOW YOU SHOULD MEASURE COACH KNIGHT. HE MAINTAINED A HIGH LEVEL OF EXCELLENCE THAT WE TAKE FOR GRANTED.[7]

—*Isiah Thomas, star on IU's national championship team of 1981*

⌒

I've done close to a thousand things to motivate kids as individuals or teams. And I'll guarantee a lot of them I wouldn't want to talk about at a church social, PTA meeting, or garden party. But we're not teaching kids how to play canasta.

HE HAS ME DOING THINGS I USED TO BELIEVE WERE IMPOSSIBLE. HE MAKES US BETTER BASKETBALL PLAYERS, BUT FIRST OF ALL, BETTER MEN. IS THAT BAD?[8]

—*John Ritter, former Indiana player*

I don't know how we won World War II because (Gen. Dwight Eisenhower) (was) one of the great vacillating individuals in world history.[9]

Knight emphasizes a point during a timeout, although this wasn't the coach at his most intense. (Indiana University Archives)

Coaches can learn a lot just
by studying examples of
indecisiveness or timidity.[10]

Coaching is motivation. Coaching is leadership. Coaching is, are you going to get the guys to attack the river? Some of them are going to get killed, but we got to go attack the river.[11]

⌒

I like decisive people. When Truman fired MacArthur, it wasn't a matter of being right or wrong. It was having the guts to do it.[12]

⌒

It was a simple decision. Why would that even be hard? . . . He made the decision with what he did. I don't think you have any recourse. Kids screw up. Kids make mistakes. But that wasn't my mistake.

—*Knight in 1996 referring to player Sherron Wilkerson, whom he dismissed from the team after Wilkerson had been charged with domestic abuse*

⌒

CBS newscaster Dan Rather is the audience this time as he gets some pointers from Knight during taping of a segment for 60 Minutes. (Indiana University Archives)

5

SUCCESS

*"A lot of people don't like to be
pushed to the limit."*

—STEVE ALFORD

People want to win. You know, people want national championship banners. People want to talk about Indiana being competitive. How do we get there? We don't get there with milk and cookies. We never have and never will.[1]

⌒

I know what my problem is. The difference between winning and losing is so great for me—such a tremendous emotional difference—that it really works at me just before we play.[2]

⌒

You build winning teams on character, not characters.[3]

⌒

I think it suffices to say that no matter what you're doing— whether it be playing defense or the fast break—discipline is a matter of making the proper choice of what to do at the proper time.[4]

⌒

Bud (Wilkinson) told me who a team plays is incidental. He said what counts is that a team strives to reach its potential every game . . . that it makes no difference if you are playing a strong team or a weak team.[5]

⌒

The single most fulfilling thing about coaching has been kids who have played for us coming back to watch us play again.[6]

⌒

Victory favors the team that makes the fewest mistakes.[7]

⌒

There are very few Jerry Wests, very few all-around players . . . I don't want guys who can't dribble the ball to dribble it, and I don't want guys who can't shoot free throws handling the ball at the end of a game. I am not an equal-opportunity coach.[8]

⌒

Discipline is such a misused word. To me, discipline is doing what you should be doing when you should be doing it, and recognizing that now is the time to do it.[9]

⌒

Looks, talent, appearance, and ability to communicate are all really good assets, especially when put together with discipline. As a coach, I would rather take a little more disciplined (player) who may not look as good as somebody else might, and think that we might stand a better chance with those people than with the less-disciplined, more-talented player.

⁓

You can win and still not succeed, still not achieve what you should.[10]

⁓

The rewards in coaching are not tied to wins and losses and championships. They are watching a former player coaching a team to a national championship. A player like Mike Krzyzewski at Duke, who I coached at Army. It's seeing a player go from basketball into something else. To articulate on television and through radio the game of basketball, concisely and accurately, as Quinn Buckner has done.[11]

—Knight upon his induction into the Basketball Hall of Fame

⁓

WHAT MAKES IT TOUGH IS THAT COACH (KNIGHT) TAKES A GENUINE
INTEREST IN YOU TO MAKE YOU A BETTER PERSON AND PLAYER. A
LOT OF PEOPLE DON'T LIKE TO BE PUSHED TO THE LIMIT. THAT'S
WHAT I RESPECT IN COACH SO MUCH.[12]

—*Steve Alford, floor leader of 1987 NCAA Championship team*

I agree with you: In any game, somebody is going to lose. But
it doesn't need to be me.[13]

—*Knight to his mother years ago*

My father (Carroll "Pat" Knight) was the most disciplined
man I ever saw. Most people, they hear the word *discipline*,
and right away they think about a whip and a chair. I have
my own definition.[14]

I'm always bothered when we can't beat the good teams.[15]

The coat rarely came off, but loosening the tie?
That's another story. (Indiana University Archives)

I can't tell you how many games (Adolph) Rupp has won, how many games Dean Smith has won. I can't tell you how many games I've won, unless I stop and think about it a little bit.

HE OWNED ME. WHEN HE GOT FOCUSED ON GAMES, HE COACHED AS WELL AS ANYONE.[16]
—*former Notre Dame coach Digger Phelps, whose Fighting Irish teams won only four of sixteen games against the Knight-coached Hoosiers*

My goal with any kid who's ever come here, is to have their parent come up to me after our last game and say, "Thank you."

Of the eighty kids who have played (and stayed at Indiana), seventy-seven have a degree. And you're going to have a hard time matching that anywhere. And among those people are teachers and lawyers—I'm not all that proud of the lawyers—and doctors and dentists and businessmen, and a hell of a lot of people that have been pretty good in representing the university after they've left.

As a team starts a schedule, each game becomes a barometer for preparing to play the next one. It's a little bit like finding that it's necessary to change from pabulum to oatmeal.[17]

⌒

If I was the raving maniac I keep reading about, I don't think we'd win so many games. And if modern kids are supposed to resent my rules about short hair and coats and ties, how come my guys win for me and then come back and help me recruit?[18]

⌒

There's a German novel that says, "People want talent, but all too often they can't accept those things that go along with it." A talented singer may be somewhat sensitive about the handling of arrangements or the use of notes, because his or her attention to detail has made that person successful. So when he gets upset about a particular arrangement, that may be one of the things upon which his very talent is based.[19]

⌒

When a coach is honored, it's an honor for all the players that played for him, and is a recognition of the teams he has had over the years. I've been fortunate to have had a lot of great kids and players at West Point and Indiana. It means a lot to me to see them all share in this kind of recognition. A player enters the Hall of Fame on his ability, a coach enters on the ability of his players.

—Knight on his being voted into the Basketball Hall of Fame

The Bobby Knight Shuffle? (Indiana University Archives)

MAN OF CONVICTION

"I'm willing to get into the arena and scratch and claw for something I believe in."

—BOB KNIGHT

I am willing to do some things that other people won't do. And a lot of them center around the word *no*.[1]

⁓

If you say no and then at some time in the future you want to change no to yes because of circumstances, then that's a good thing; everybody's tickled that you now say you will. But if you say, "Yes, I will," and two days later you find out, "No, I can't," then everyone's upset because you told them you would and now you say you won't. The word *no* to me is the most powerful word in the English language, not for its effect on others but for how it affects you.[2]

⁓

I can't change. I'm not very flexible. I've tried to study this game. I've tried to understand it. I've tried to study right and wrong. I've spent a lot of time on it. And I have to continue to do what I believe is right.[3]

⁓

I've often said this to some of the most sanctimonious self-righteous critics that I have. I would hope when Judgment Day comes, they don't have to appear before Saint Peter's table with me and only one space available for both of us and the judgment being made on which of us has done the most for his fellow man. I have no doubt Saint Peter will turn to me and say, "Robert, pass through the gate."[4]

I'm an anachronism. I'm twenty years behind the times. What (Vince) Lombardi did twenty years ago, people look at it differently today. I'm more demanding than anyone else, and I think this is not an era or time of demands. This is a time of acquiescence. I'm out of step with the times.[5]

I don't believe there's a lot of gray area. The only gray is the thin line that separates black from white. That's a very, very thin line.[6]

America, America, God shed his grace on thee.
      —*"The best eight words put together in the English language,"*
      according to a speech Knight gave at an August 1989 seminar

⌒

If I had my way, I think you know we wouldn't be playing late-night ESPN games . . . I think it's absolutely asinine that you people supporting your basketball team here, to do so, have to come to Assembly Hall at nine o'clock at night. Basketball should be a game that you can have a lot of fun with—come in at seven o'clock, see the basketball game. You've got time to go somewhere and get something to eat. You've got time to study or to do whatever you people do.[7]

⌒

UNFORTUNATELY, THIS IS BIG BUSINESS . . . I THINK THE KIDS CAN ADJUST TO IT. LIFE IS NOT ALL UTOPIA, BABY. LIFE IS ADJUSTMENTS.
      —*Dick Vitale, ESPN college basketball commentator*

⌒

The only thing I think boycotting the Olympics [in 1980] would do is take away the opportunity to kick the hell out of the Russians and a lot of other people that it wouldn't displease me as an American to see the hell kicked out of. I think what we ought to do is take away the television money from the Russians by not showing any of the Games back here on live TV as the first priority. Secondly, I believe our government should put an embargo on travel to Russia—to prevent American spectators from spending the millions of dollars they would otherwise spend in Moscow at the Games. What better way to stick it to the Russians than to beat them and not pay them at the same time?[8]

I can guarantee you there isn't a coaches' association meeting tonight in the Soviet Union.[9]

—Knight in a speech to the National Conference of High School Coaches and Officials

I think basketball is fun for me because I haven't changed very much. I think some people perhaps don't feel that it is, because they've had to change with the times, you know, and I'm almost obsolete and way behind the times.[10]

Anytime that you feel that you've had to do something a certain way rather than, "This is the way we want to do it," or "the way we should do it," then I think it becomes a little bit of a problem for you.[11]

I've always been too confrontational, especially when I know I'm right. I know as well as anybody does: I have to develop a more diplomatic approach. I'm not very good at just forgetting something and going on, and I'm truly sorry about that.

—*Knight in a May 13, 2000, prepared statement he made while IU administrators discussed his situation, giving birth to the infamous zero-tolerance dictum for him*

Knight talking about the controversial 1979 Pan-American Games in Puerto Rico, where he coached the United States men's basketball team to a gold medal amid the hoopla surrounding his physical confrontation with a security guard:

An international tea is a situation for diplomacy. Basketball is not an international tea. It's competition, and we didn't go there (Puerto Rico) to apologize or take any crap off anybody.[12]

BOBBY IS REALLY GETTING ROASTED BACK IN THE STATES. PEOPLE UP THERE HAVE NO IDEA WHAT A ZOO IT IS DOWN HERE AND WHAT A GREAT JOB HE'S DOING.[13]

—Michigan State coach Jud Heathcote sticking up for Knight during the 1979 Pan-Am Games

I clapped when Puerto Rico got the silver medal for second place. That's how I feel about the whole place—it's second rate.[14]

I AM STRONGLY IN SUPPORT OF BOBBY KNIGHT. I AM NOT ABOUT TO
SIGN EXTRADITION PAPERS.[15]

> —*Otis Bowen, Indiana governor, following the fiasco in*
> *Puerto Rico during the 1979 Pan-American Games*

That whole thing has never done anything but amaze me,
because anybody who was there knew that what I said, and
what our players said, was exactly the way it happened.[16]

I don't particularly look favorably on a group of people who
are United States citizens, who don't pay any taxes, who
received tremendous amounts in welfare and who got approximately $10 million in aid to put those games on in the first
place, booing the national anthem.[17]

> —*Knight referring to booing fans in Puerto Rico*
> *after the Pan-American championship game*

I suppose some people don't like the way I represent the U.S. The hell with 'em. I'm willing to get into the arena and scratch and claw for something I believe in. I want to see the U.S. represented in a winning manner and not be stepped on.[18]

~

I don't smoke, I don't drink, and I don't advertise it. I also don't go to church, but I think I possess far more Christian values than a lot of people who go to church every week. I'm not proud of the fact that I use profanities, but my language is my language, and I don't apologize for it.[19]

~

People are always thinking about how they'd like to be remembered, and when I'm done coaching and I leave Indiana University, whether they've liked me or disliked me, there are going to be two things they are going to be able to say about me: Number one is that I was honest, and number two is that I kissed no man's (behind). I can't mold myself to what other people want me to be.[20]

~

I strongly opposed President Carter's decision not to send American athletes to Moscow (in 1980 for the Summer Olympics). I felt that we were taking away one of our great strengths—showing people all over the world just how our kids compete, how hard they work on behalf of the United States.[21]

Guys who apologize for things in public always amaze me. When I read how somebody apologized publicly for something, I never think there's much sincerity in that. Or when I read that somebody has donated $10,000—I've donated a hell of a lot of money to things, and nobody knows anything about them, and nobody will ever know about them. I just think that the things that you do privately are much more meaningful.[22]

People have an appreciation for someone who says what he thinks. I think they know that I make mistakes but try to do what's right. At least I hope so.[23]

If you do what you have to do and do it right, you're going to win.[24]

I always know what I'm doing.[25]

I believe first and foremost I am an honest man. If I like you, I will be with you all the way. If I don't, you know about it from the start.[26]

Knight learned some of his lessons on the game of basketball at West Point—while sitting down. (United States Military Academy photo)

THE GAME OF
BASKETBALL

"It's ironic, but one of the things that kept him from playing more in college was his defense."

—JOHN HAVLICEK

Basketball is American, it's hot dogs, popcorn, and "The Star-Spangled Banner."[1]

My philosophy is that to beat the game, you have to understand it. To respect it, but not be afraid of it. Once you understand the game, the variables become the players. I tell my players, "You're not playing Michigan or Illinois. You're playing the game of basketball. Your opponent is yourself, your potential."[2]

Basketball is a game of movement.[3]

SOME MEN PREPARE TEAMS WELL AND SOME ARE GOOD BENCH COACHES. BOBBY DOES BOTH. IT'S UNBELIEVABLE HOW HE STAYS UP FOR PRACTICE EVERY DAY. NO MISTAKE GOES UNCORRECTED.[4]

—*Fred Taylor*

Boys, we talk a lot about teamwork. You black guys who understand music and rhythm allow two white guys in on it. I'm really impressed. That makes me very happy.[5]

—Knight after five of his players presented him a cake on his fifty-fourth birthday

Basketball is mental as to physical as four is to one.[6]

You make a critical mistake in looking at film from a positive standpoint. It's the mistakes that are going to win or lose the ballgames, not the positive plays.

I coached 152 games at Army, and we played only twenty minutes of zone defense.[7]

The individual habits of a man defense have historically differed distinctly from the individual habits of a man playing zone defense.[8]

⌒

I have a very simple approach to the game. We start our players off on the defensive end of it. Defense is emphasized from the very beginning. From there, we go to offense and stress the importance of getting the best shot you can. Then you stress execution, nothing fancy, just execution.

⌒

A defensive man must be constantly turning his head.[9]

⌒

We changed the style of play. Indiana had not been a defensive type of team. They ran a lot and shot a lot, and we changed that. I think the favorite cry from the stands when I first came here was "Shoot! Shoot! Shoot!" Then I guess they figured out after a while we weren't going to shoot all that much.[10]

—Knight referring to the "Hurryin' Hoosiers" style of basketball that preceded his arrival there in 1971

⌒

Defense is an attitude.

IT'S IRONIC, BUT ONE OF THE THINGS THAT KEPT HIM FROM PLAYING MORE IN COLLEGE WAS HIS DEFENSE. HE WASN'T A VERY GOOD DEFENSIVE PLAYER BECAUSE HE WASN'T QUICK ENOUGH. HE WORKED HARD AT IT, BUT HE ALWAYS SEEMED TO END UP FOULING SOMEONE. NOW HIS TEAMS ARE KNOWN FOR THEIR DEFENSE—MAYBE HE FELT THAT IF THAT WAS SOMETHING HE COULDN'T DO HIMSELF, HE'D GO OUT AND GET PLAYERS WHO COULD.[11]

—John Havlicek, one of Knight's teammates at Ohio State in the early sixties

There is no point in the game more critical than the initial minutes of the second half.[12]

It is not what your opponents do, but what you do that is going to win the games.[13]

The will to prepare to win is more important than the will to win.[14]

We're always looking for new ways to do things. I'm forever drawing up diagrams. Every day, every practice. We try everything. Some of my ideas are pretty good, but some are pretty bad . . . But when they work in a game, when you see the players execute what they've been working on—there's no finer feeling in the world.[15]

The hardest part of my job is waiting to play—the final preparation. Once the game starts, I'm fine.[16]

When I first started, I had the idea that it was a battle each night between the referees and myself. I really think I've gotten away from that . . . I have found that the more officiating you do, the less coaching.[17]

Don't make two consecutive cuts in the same direction.[18]
—*excerpt from* IU's Offensive and Defensive System, *a four-page document that was made available to every college and high school coach in the country*

Knight has often been as emphatic in making a point during practice as he is during a game. (Guy Zimmer photo, Indiana University Photographic Services)

If you want to do your own thing, if you want to play your own game—at Indiana, we're going to play my game.[19]

~

We've worked very hard with our kids, getting them into position on blocking-charging situations, and when I think they did it right, I'll back them.[20]

~

We're screening to get a shot. To run our offense with the kind of efficiency that we've had and the kind of shooting percentage that we've had over the years, we've had to have a lot of pretty good screening. Because that's what gets us our shots.[21]

~

HE'S A REAL TEACHER OF TIMING ON OFFENSE. I'M ENVIOUS OF THAT TALENT OF HIS. IT'S SOMETHING VERY DIFFICULT TO CONVEY, BUT HE DOES IT TO PERFECTION.
        —*Tates Locke, Army's head coach before Knight took over for him*

~

Some people might think I don't believe in the fast break. That's not true. I like an "intelligent" running game, and the most effective fast breaks are those that come off an opponent's turnovers—and those are caused by the defense.

The average coach wants his team to score points. It's his character, his machismo, whatever you want to call it, that's at stake. So if I make a coach concerned enough about my defense stopping his offense, then he'll forget about my offense.[22]

Knight on three things during the course of a game most likely to get him out of his seat:
Defensively, when a player doesn't recognize where the ball is; when he misses something because he didn't know where the ball was, which is paramount. That's one thing. A second thing is missing a block-out. The third is not moving—to help out or to impede the progress of the ball.[23]

When I get on an official, it's because I think he's doing a lousy job. I don't have time to sit there and figure out how I can "work" an official. I've never done that.[24]

∽

To me what's most enjoyable is the practice and preparation.[25]

∽

One of the biggest wastes of practice time is a "free" shooting period. In free shooting, players approximate positions that are too far removed from game conditions.[26]

∽

I do dumb things sometimes.[27]

∽

There are too many things I have yet to explore about the game of basketball.[28]

—Upon his firing in September 2000

∽

KNIGHT HIS
OWNSELF

"Listen to me. Listen to me, Bobby . . ."

—WOODY HAYES

There are a lot of times, too, when I feel like I'm a lone ship on a stormy sea and I don't have any sail.[1]

⌒

BOB REMINDS ME OF ALEXANDER THE GREAT, WHO CONQUERED THE WORLD AND THEN SAT DOWN AND CRIED BECAUSE THERE WAS NOTHING LEFT TO CONQUER.[2]

—Al McGuire

⌒

Maybe I've forgotten this, but I don't think I've ever shot anybody. Maybe I've forgotten that, maybe there's somebody along the way I've shot, but I don't remember.[3]

⌒

Let him who is without sin cast the first reprimand.[4]
—Knight quoting his so-called John 8:7 rule

⌒

I'd like to be left alone,
just to coach basketball.[5]

BOBBY IS DRIVEN BY A FORCE GREATER THAN ANY COACH I'VE EVER KNOWN. NOBODY COULD KEEP THAT PACE WITHOUT IT REFLECTING IN HIS FACE AND EMOTIONS.[6]

—Fred Taylor

A lot of my problem is just too many people don't go beyond countenances.[7]

LISTEN TO ME. LISTEN TO ME, BOBBY, BECAUSE I'VE MADE A LOT OF MISTAKES AND YOU DON'T HAVE TO REPEAT MINE.[8]

—Woody Hayes, speaking to Knight

We didn't trade shoves. I did all the shoving.[9]
—Knight referring to his memorable encounter with an LSU fan at the 1981 Final Four, when he stuffed the annoying fan into a garbage can

I probably ignore ten thousand things for every one that I get upset about. But I'll be damned if I'll take that in a public place.[10]

I did not kick my son. You see, I love my son.[11]
> —*Knight referring to an incident during a 1993 game against Notre Dame, when he kicked his player-son Pat's chair in anger*

Whatever I do is magnified, and I have done some dumb things.[12]

Sure I have a temper. But I don't think that's bad. It's when a temper controls the person, instead of the person controlling the temper, that I think a problem exists.[13]

Not even the fashion police could stop Bobby Knight from doing things his own way. (Indiana University Archives)

If we chastised every person in history who was temperamental, we might have had very little progress.[14]

⁓

THERE WAS A TIME WHEN IT WAS A COMPLIMENT TO CALL HIM JEKYLL AND HYDE. BUT NOW HE'LL COME HOME AFTER A GAME AND ASK ME, "HOW DID I BEHAVE TONIGHT?"[15]

—Nancy Knight, the coach's first wife

⁓

He was just killing bugs. You can't believe how many are walking in front of our bench.

—Knight explaining why assistant Dave Bliss angrily threw a towel to the floor in front of the bench, eliciting a warning from an official

⁓

I don't think I'm arbitrary; I don't make endless unilateral decisions. There are things I adjust to. I'll adjust to my kids. That's not violating discipline.[16]

⁓

When I first came here, I think I took what I was doing with probably too great a degree of importance. I think one of the great turning points for me was to find things that would have, at some point, really antagonized me to be relatively amusing (now). I think that's really helped me a lot.[17]

I let some personal feelings outweigh good judgment as far as the general scope of things in that particular game were concerned.[18]

   —*After pulling his team off the court with about fifteen minutes left in a game against the Soviet Union and the Hoosiers trailing, 66-43*

HE'S THE MOST INTENSELY DRIVEN MAN I'VE EVER MET.[19]

   —*John Feinstein, author of* A Season on the Brink

I am certain that what I did in tossing the chair was an embarrassment to Indiana University . . . While I certainly take exception to criticism on who I start or play in any game, I feel a criticism of my action in throwing the chair (in a 1985 Indiana-Purdue game) is justifiable. It's something that I will not let happen again.[20]

I heard this little voice yelling, "Bob, Bob," and the only one I saw was the sweet little old lady. Finally, she said, "If you're not going to sit down, would you throw your chair over here?"[21]

AT TIMES I WAS REALLY TEED OFF AT HIM WHEN I PLAYED AT ARMY. AT TIMES I REALLY SAW A RED FLAG WHEN I SAW HIM. BUT EVERYONE RESPECTS HIM. THEY KNOW HE'S WORKING HARDER THAN THEY ARE.[22]
—*Mike Krzyzewski, longtime Duke head coach and one of Knight's players at West Point*

I just don't have a personality that connotes humor. It kills me. I get castigated for screaming at some ref. And the other coach? Oh, he's perfect, he's being deified, and I know he's one of the worst cheaters in the country. It's like I tell my players: Your biggest opponent isn't the other guy. It's human nature.[23]

People are always surprised when they hear about my fishing. Everybody thinks I'm so wound up I'm going to have to leave in five minutes. But I don't carry over that stuff you see on the court. There's nothing I enjoy more than winding down some river, floating along, watching for deer, counting the squirrels. And nobody knows what you've done that day except you and the guys involved.[24]

BOBBY WAS QUITE A SPLIT PERSONALITY. THERE WERE TIMES WHEN WE WERE GOOD FRIENDS AND, THEN, LIKE THAT, TIMES WHEN HE WOULDN'T EVEN TALK TO ME.[25]

—John Havlicek

My manners set me apart in a little cocoon, and that's something that's very beneficial to me.[26]

Practically all of us have some problem to deal with in life. For some, it's something as simple as meeting people or talking in front of people. My temper problem is a lot more troublesome than those, and it's something I've had to deal with for as long as I can remember.

—Knight in a May 13, 2000, statement he prepared while IU administrators discussed his situation, giving birth to the infamous zero-tolerance dictum for him

Christ had a temper. Christ destroyed the tables in the temple, so when you start talking about people who have a temper, I think you have to start there. Don't misunderstand me. I'm not trying to draw any parallels between myself and Christ.[27]

⌒

Intense, *demand*, and *temper* have been a three-braided rope for me, and I really believe that the first two have been a major reason for the success of our kids and teams. It's my job and my determination to temper that third braid.

⌒

I made the comment that I'd always prided myself in going from Point A to Point B unless somewhere in between sat the Board of Trustees. I thought it was kind of a comical remark.[28]

—Knight referring to a joke he had cracked at one of his wife Karen's cancer benefits

⌒

I HOPE WHAT HE JUST DID WON'T BE TERMED INAPPROPRIATE PHYSI-
CAL CONTACT.[29]

> —*Karen Knight, after husband Bob Knight kissed her during his*
> *emotional farewell speech to IU students in September 2000*

I don't expect everybody to agree with everything I do or say.
I mean, hell, my mom didn't. I remember two girls that I went
to high school with met my mom at a counter in a grocery
store in my hometown of Orrville, in northeastern Ohio, and
these two girls said to my mom, "You know, Indiana plays on
TV Saturday, Hazel. Are you going to watch it?" And she
said, "Well, I'm not sure. I just hope he behaves." Well, I'm
sure at times I disappointed my mother in that regard.

The last time we beat Kentucky was way, way back before I was a grandfather. I got to thinking it was before I was a father, it was so long ago. I spoke at a clinic down in Lexington for Converse this summer, and my opening line was if there was something here that somebody has that you can come up here and we can play quickly that I can beat you at . . . We haven't won for so damn long down here against anybody, so I'd like to go home this summer having won something. Maybe we could throw a ball at the waste basket or something.

—*Knight following IU's 83-75 victory over Kentucky in December 1999*

I love long hair and beards and mustaches. Yes, sir. If you want to look like you want to look, dress like you want to dress, act like you want to act, play like you want to play, shoot like you want to shoot, do your own thing, I say great. But you're sure as hell not coming to Indiana to play basketball. At Indiana, we're going to do my thing.[30]

Knight does have a good sense of humor, even when it comes to basketball. (Bryan Spurlock photo)

There are too many rabbits around. I know that. But it doesn't do me any good. Instead of fighting the elephants, I just keep going after the rabbits.[31]

~

When I grabbed Jimmy Wisman by the shirt on national TV, the first person that said anything about it was Jimmy Wisman's mother. She said, "If I had been there, I would have grabbed him, too."[32]

~

You remember when you were a kid growing up and believed in Santa Claus? There's not much difference between Claus and me today, you know. We're two overweight, lovable guys that kids really enjoy.[33]

~

Responding to critics of hunting, a sport he cherishes:
The lifespan of a quail is thirteen months. I never hunt deer or anything else; I hunt quail, and quail have to be thinned out for new broods. There are people who abuse hunting, but it is a very essential part of the natural balance.[34]

~

A man's got to believe in something. I believe I'll go fishing.

—*Sign over Knight's private office door.*

I never worry about somebody I either don't know or don't respect.[35]

⌒

Everyone who visits here
Brings happiness.
Some coming in
Some going out.

—Sign over Knight's office at Assembly Hall

⌒

I enjoy being by myself. I don't get any pleasure out of being around a bunch of people I don't know. Cocktail parties are impossible for me to take, especially the inane chatter of so many women.[36]

⌒

If I go to a restaurant and order dinner and it's lousy, that doesn't spoil my evening. It's just a lousy dinner, so I don't eat it. Let's get on with what else we're going to do. But if we go to a basketball game and play a lousy game—yes, that spoils my evening.[37]

⌒

HE DOESN'T CHEAT. HE DOESN'T DRINK. HE DOESN'T EVEN CHASE
WOMEN. BUT FOR SOME REASON HE THINKS HE HAS BEEN A BAD BOY,
AND NO MATTER HOW SUCCESSFUL HE BECOMES, HE THINKS HE
MUST BE PUNISHED.[38]

> —*Roy Bates, a high school basketball coach at one of
> Knight's rival schools, later hired as a Knight assistant*

It amazed me in this TV—give me a word I can use. I don't
want to dignify it by calling it a presentation or a production
. . . Tell me, what's an unnamed source? Is an unnamed
source me standing up here and saying that I was just told
outside by somebody who doesn't want to be identified that
65 percent of the men in this room are having extramarital
affairs with sheep? Is that an unnamed source?

> —*referring to CNN/SI piece in which Neil Reed accused
> Knight of choking him during a practice*

President Myles Brand, in a meeting with me, gave me a set of guidelines he expects me to follow if I want to continue as IU's basketball coach. I have absolutely no problem with the guidelines. The establishment of effective and proper guidelines can in the long run help me become a better coach. As I have said before, I recognize that I have a problem with my temper. For those times my situation has ever caused me to do anything to give anyone understandable and testifiable reason to be upset, I am sincerely sorry.[39]

—Knight in a prepared statement

I hope that when I retire I'll have enough assistants in head jobs so I can live anywhere I want and still have a place nearby where I can go over and help out.[40]

GENERAL

STUFF

"Coach Knight has never been a man who pampered anybody."

—SCOTT MAY

ACCOUNTABILITY

Today, kids are always getting off the hook—someone is always finding a reason where they don't have to take responsibility for their actions, and that's wrong. I'm held accountable for everything I do, and they should be, too.[1]

ADAPTABILITY

Our team is like a ball of putty. It is always changing form. We might look one way for Iowa, then we roll the putty around and look a little different for Michigan. After Michigan, we'll work it around again and have still another look for Purdue. When you get down to it, that's the joy of this game.[2]

AGENTS

These poor, dumb kids give some jerk 7 percent for negotiating a contract that the kid is going to get anyhow. If schools really wanted to do something to help these kids, they should provide a legal expert (a local attorney or a law school graduate) to help them with contracts. Instead, we have these parasites who have no interest in the kids other than trying to turn a fast buck.[3]

ALUMNI

I really think that most problems are created by alumni who are unable to brag about their school's football and basketball teams.[4]

∽

Some guy says, "I'm tired of our getting beat. We'd better start cheating to get us some players."[5]

∽

Our alumni are scared to death of me. I've got them in a position where I don't utilize them. I don't expect them to contribute to basketball. We pay our own way.[6]

—*Knight in a benefit speech for the Knox County Youth Shelter*

∽

BABIES

THOSE WHO LEFT WERE BABIES. NONE OF THEM UNDERSTOOD WHAT IT WAS ALL ABOUT. THEY THOUGHT IT WOULD BE LIKE HIGH SCHOOL. ALL THEIR LIVES THEY WERE STARS AND WERE TREATED THAT WAY. BUT COACH KNIGHT HAS NEVER BEEN A MAN WHO PAMPERED ANYBODY, SO THEY RAN FOR THEIR LIVES.[7]

—*Scott May*

∽

COMMUNITY

Athletics, to be more than athletics, has to be a contributor to a university. It has to be a contributor to a community. A team that just plays without involvement with people isn't really what I think of when I think of what's best in intercollegiate athletics.

DRUGS

I think we should attack the drug problem. We should go after them. We've got commando units; we've got Green Berets, the Navy has SEALs, we've probably got ultra-secret units we don't know anything about. Let's just turn them loose and eradicate it. To me, that's the answer and the only answer.[8]

Drugs in this generation are just a substitute for the alcoholism when I was growing up.[9]

Think about people who should be more successful and why they aren't. They can't handle drugs and they can't handle alcohol. Nobody can.[10]

EDUCATION

Athletes under the right direction are willing to work as hard, put as much effort forth, as they ever were. But the people who administer the athletes are less demanding. Teachers as a whole have changed—the scope of education is far less demanding today than it was twenty years ago—and that's a tragic mistake.[11]

We need a minor league for kids to go to right out of high school who don't have the academic ability. We try to make every kid into a college student. Let's forget how much money is involved and think about the kid and his education.[12]

—Knight in a speech to the National Conference of High School Coaches and Officials

INTEGRITY

HE JUST DOESN'T CHEAT. NEVER. HE DOESN'T RATIONALIZE. INSTEAD, WHAT HE DOES DO IS THE SINGLE-MOST IMPORTANT THING IN COACHING. HE TURNS OUT KIDS WHO ARE READY FOR SOCIETY.[13]

—Pete Newell

INTELLECT

HIS INTELLIGENCE IS DIRECTED LIKE A LASER ON A NARROW AREA
WHERE NOT MANY INTELLECTS HAVE TRAVELED.[14]

—*Bob Hammel, Knight confidante and former*
Bloomington Herald-Telephone *sports columnist*

LOYALTY

FROM THE FIRST DAY I MET HIM, I KNEW HE WAS A GREAT STUDENT.
NOW HE'S BECOME A GREAT TEACHER. I WOULD NEVER IN A MILLION
YEARS CRITICIZE HIM FOR HIS TEMPER. THAT'S REALLY JUST A
FACADE. HE'S AS LOYAL A PERSON AS YOU'LL EVER KNOW.[15]

—*Tates Locke*

MALCONTENTS

It seems like some kind of malcontent always has something
to say. I don't know why Indiana was picked for something
like this. Because I think you could go to any school in
America and you could find kids that were bitter, that were
unhappy, that were malcontents.

NATIONAL POLLS

I don't care whether we're ranked first or fiftieth or not at all. As long as we're doing the things we've worked on and the things I know can help make us a good team, then that's what is satisfying.

~

NBA

I never even watch the pros. If the NBA was on channel 5 and a bunch of frogs were making love on channel 4, I'd watch the frogs, even if they came in fuzzy.[16]

~

On his prospects of ever coaching in the NBA:
I'd be a very poor one. I need time to prepare, time to think things through. I need kids that respond to roles. I don't think I'd be a positive influence.

~

If they establish a pro team at Fort Knox, and if my salary is what I can carry out of the vault, I'm not going.[17]

~

NCAA

We think of the NCAA as this monster that exists in Kansas City. All Kansas City is, is an administrative body for the NCAA. Any investigative body in the world needs the power of subpoena and the threat of prosecution to be successful. The NCAA has neither.[18]

The way it is structured, the NCAA is powerless. The NCAA has to vote on everything that is done . . . You can't investigate and you can't punish without those two conditions. It doesn't matter who you are. J. Edgar Hoover could not have solved anything without those basic powers.[19]

PEOPLE

I'm very, very partial to that part of the country (Indiana) to begin with, yet I've really enjoyed living here, and the people here have been very good. But there have been changes here that affect things and affect thinking, and people are always, I think, the key to success.

—Knight in 1988 regarding rumors that he might leave IU to take the New Mexico job, not long after Thomas Ehrlich had replaced Knight's friend John Ryan as school president

There are enough people that are going to screw things up that if you just learn about yourself you've got a chance of being better.[20]

∾

People always make things different. See, that's the big difference for me in the last four or five years as opposed to prior to that. Bear Bryant once said you have to have an ironclad contract to protect yourself from a time when the president would lose his guts. And I think what he was referring to then was that people would change. And I've seen that. I had five years at West Point that I really enjoyed, and one year just wasn't particularly enjoyable because the people that were making decisions had changed.[21]

∾

I'm impressed with people when they stand up to me. When they don't, I have very little respect for them. Particularly when they're right and I'm wrong. Sometimes I know I'm wrong and they're right, and I challenge them just because I'm interested in seeing what they'll do.[22]

∾

I don't like people very well, because most of them lack intestinal fortitude or they lack integrity.[23]

∾

PERCEPTIONS

Spend a week at our practices, not just an hour or even a couple of days; you'll be amazed how different things are from some perceptions. Billy Packer and Dick Vitale, who may watch more college practices than anybody, both called to say that I would rank down the list as far as coaches who get tough with players.[24]

PERSEVERANCE

YOU OUGHTA KNOW THAT I'M THE ONE THAT BUILT BOBBY KNIGHT'S DOGHOUSE. I'M THE ONE THAT PUT IT TOGETHER LAYER BY LAYER BY LAYER. THERE WERE TIMES THAT COACH KNIGHT AND I DIDN'T REALLY GET ALONG. THERE WERE TIMES THAT I EVEN THOUGHT OF QUITTING, AND THANK GOD I DIDN'T.[25]

—Landon Turner, former IU player who was partially paralyzed after he broke his neck in a mishap. Knight started the Landon Turner Trust Fund, which raised more than $300,000 on Turner's behalf.

POINT SPREADS

I just don't understand how point spreads can be listed in the newspapers—it defies my understanding. That is being an accessory to something that is illegal.[26]

PSYCHOLOGY

There is so much more psychology now that says you shouldn't interfere with a kid's development with any rules at all. Let the kid do this and let the kid do that. I think that's bull.[27]

⌒

REALITY

Everybody wants to be a pro, yet the percentage of kids who can do it is infinitesimal. Somewhere between that decision and facing reality has to come the idea of preparing yourself to do something other than play basketball.[28]

⌒

I'm not a believer in striving for the impossible. No. I'm a believer in being very realistic about what you can and cannot do, and then trying to achieve what you realistically can achieve.[29]

⌒

ROLE MODELS

I don't think everybody can set a perfect example in every single way. I don't think any person can be all things to all people.[30]

⌒

RULES

I'm really against that (paying scholarship athletes a monthly stipend). I think the payment for a college athlete comes in the right environment, from the exposure he gets to all kinds of things way beyond what the normal college students gets . . . One of the arguments is if we give kids a hundred dollars a month, that will eliminate a lot of the cheating. But it won't eliminate the people who want to give him two hundred dollars a month. There's no way that's going to work. That would be like pouring a pound of salt in the Pacific.[31]

SATISFACTION

Victory has never been a particularly satisfying thing to me. It's really hard for me to say, "Well, we won."[32]

SPORTSWRITERS

It was fun having you here. I'll tell you what it's like. It's like reading Shakespeare all your life, then suddenly being confronted with Donald Duck.[33]

—Knight to a departing reporter following an interview

Nobody's telling me to write new paragraphs or how to spell words. Or that I'm writing abut the wrong guys. I don't have seventeen thousand people telling me how to write. I wouldn't mind being one of you guys. But I'd like to be a lot smarter than most of you.

—*in a guest column during the 1987 NCAA Tournament for the* Indianapolis News

All of us learn to write in the second grade . . . most of us go on to greater things.

I honestly don't think a lot of people in your business or mine care about athletics.

There are all those reporters and broadcasters calling from around the country who don't know the names of our players or even who we meet next. I've been tempted to make up some names or tell them our defensive success should be credited to our changing zone defenses, but I haven't. As soon as we get beat, they'll quit calling and move on to the next coach who is No. 1, so I don't take it too seriously from my standpoint.[34]

—*Knight in January 1975 after IU had reached No. 1 for the first time under him*

I CAN'T UNDERSTAND WHAT THE HANG-UP IS. I BELIEVE BOBBY WILL ANSWER ANY INTELLIGENT QUESTION.[35]

—Al McGuire, *legendary basketball coach and TV analyst*

Those were the days, my friend: Knight and Al McGuire yuk it up for the NBC television audience. (Indiana University Archives)

TIME MANAGEMENT

The most important commodity we have is time. If you're
not intelligent, time escapes you. Time has to be understood,
just like the game. Or else it will beat you.[36]

TOUGHNESS

It's an old Ohio State drill. A lot of hacking and fouling.
Havlicek put seven stitches in my eyebrow during one of
those things. They sewed me up on the training table and I
finished the practice. You didn't get a lot of sympathy there
either. Pain is a state of mind.[37]

*—referring to a drill in which three men go under a basket, a manager tosses
a ball against the backboard, and the three fight for the rebound.
Whoever gets it then has to go back up for a shot.*

You have to be discriminately tough and hard-nosed. To be
indiscriminately tough is to be wild. Perhaps the outstanding
thing about a great punishing player is his ability to absorb
punishment. They go together.[38]

APPENDIX A

Coach Knight's statement, released September 9, 1979, by Indiana University, regarding the 1979 incident in Puerto Rico involving Knight and a security guard:

At approximately 9:50 A.M. on the morning of July 8, the United States Pan-American basketball team arrived by municipal bus at the gymnasium of Holy Spirit High School in San Juan for a 10:00 A.M. workout in preparation for a game that night with Canada. As we turned the corner, I saw a yellow bus parked in front of the gym and assumed that another team was working out at that time.

When our bus stopped, I told one of my assistant coaches, Mike Krzyzewski, to go into the gym to see if that was the case and to find out when they would be done. Everyone else remained on the bus. Mike came back and told us that a policeman had said the Canadian women's team was on the floor and we could not get into the gym until ten. We stayed on the bus until a couple minutes before ten when the players, coaches, and our trainer went to the door of the gym. We stayed there for a couple of minutes until we were admitted. We went into the gym and, since our players were already dressed in practice uniforms, they only had to put on their shoes and we started our workout.

The Canadian women left the floor, showered, and changed clothes. For the first twenty minutes of our practice, the Canadians were walking through the gym as they left the shower room to go outside. One of the Canadian coaches spent several minutes watching Coach (Fred) Taylor go over the zone defense that we planned to use that night against Canada. The Canadians were very quiet and respectful of our practice as we had been of theirs.

At 10:45 I stopped our workout and we shot free throws for three minutes. I then got the entire team together in the area of the free-throw line at the opposite end of the floor from the entrance. We were going through the last-minute aspects of both our offense and defense with the players' taking notes, when I heard a commotion at the other end of the floor. I turned and saw that it was the Brazilian women's team. I recognized the coach, whom I knew, and they were all dressed in the green and gold uniform of Brazil.

I continued to talk to the players until the noise and commotion by the Brazilian women became so loud that I turned and said to their coach, "You are either going to have to be quiet or get the hell out of here," to which the Brazilian coach nodded his head in an indication that they would be quiet.

By this time Mike Krzyzewski had gone down to see the policeman, Jose de Silva, who had let us into the gym. (This was the first time at any workout we had held in eleven days in Puerto Rico that a policeman was involved with either practice times or the use of the facility.) Mike and the policeman were involved in an argument. The first words I heard were the policeman saying, "They stay here because I say they stay here." At this point I turned and walked up the floor and told him that I would like to know why we were required to wait outside until our practice time started, and the Brazilian women's team was allowed to enter the gym ten minutes before our time had expired.

He said that everyone should respect him because he was a policeman, that he was the man in charge and that we should all do what he said. I told him that the fact that he was a policeman wasn't the issue but that the time allotted to us for our practice was. Both the policeman and I talked to each other in what was much louder than a conversational tone of voice, as was the case with the policeman and Mike.

The policeman, Mike, and I came together about fifteen feet across the ten-second line on the end of the court where our players were standing. We were approximately ten feet in from the sideline. Mike was facing the team, and the policeman and I were facing each other approximately a foot apart. My hands were at my side, and the policeman was shouting and waving his hand in my face in a series of stabbing motions. On the third or fourth such motion, the policeman struck the lower portion of my right eye.

Being struck in the eye caused me to turn my head to the right, and in a purely reflex action I brought my open left hand up to push his hand aside, but, instead, my hand unintentionally came to rest on his right cheek. Since my eyes were momentarily closed at the time and my head was turned, I remember feeling his flesh and whiskers. I pushed him away and Mike stepped between us as the policeman shouted I was under arrest.

I turned and walked toward the team to get them on the bus so that we could avoid anything further. The policeman continued to shout that I was under arrest. By this time Coach Taylor was standing beside me as the policeman said he was taking me outside where I would then be sent to jail. I told him that he had no reason to place me under arrest since he had hit me in the eye to begin with, and I had done nothing but push him away from me after that had happened. He kept telling me that I was under arrest, and I kept telling him that he had hit me in the eye. Our discussion took place as the policeman, Coach Taylor, and I walked across the floor and out of the gym.

When we got outside the gym, I asked the policeman if he would like to talk this thing over and settle it before it went any further. He refused to do so, continuing to say that I was under arrest and going to jail. With that, Coach Taylor and I walked across the street to a courtyard where there were two cars parked. I leaned against one of the cars and the policeman got into the other one, which I assumed was his private automobile. He put on a hat and walked around the car, where Coach Taylor and I were leaning, and approached us with a billy club in his hand. He came up in front of me and raised the club, touching me twice on the nose, and said, "God—— you, brother, this is what I would like to use on you."

I had my arms folded and remained in that position and said, "You do whatever you think you should do." He walked away and momentarily came back, raising the club again in front of me and said, "You just want me to hit you, don't you?" I repeated the same thing: "You do whatever you think you should do."

Coach Taylor had already asked to use a telephone and was told by the policeman that there were no phones available. A police car that the policeman had called for with a walkie-talkie arrived, and I was taken to it. At no time prior to this, or after, was I ever advised of my rights. Coach Taylor tried to get into the police car with me and was pushed away by the policeman. He asked where I was being taken and the policeman refused to tell him. At this point, a nun appeared on the balcony on the courtyard calling to Coach Taylor offering him the use of a telephone.

I got into the police car as the policeman took out a notebook, which was the first time I had seen it, and walked back to the entrance of the gym and proceeded to write things in the book while talking to a few Puerto Ricans who were standing at the entrance. I assumed that he was getting their names and addresses. Mike Krzyzewski, in the meantime, asked the driver of the police car where they would be taking me. He was most cooperative and told Mike. This was something that I later noted when discussing the incident with the lieutenant at the district police office. The policeman who had arrested me returned to the car, opened the back door and put handcuffs on me.

I was then taken to the police station at Hato Rey, which was very close to the Pan-American Village as was the gymnasium where we were practicing. At the police station I was put into a cell. As this was being done, I held my hands up to the arresting policeman, asking if he was going to take the handcuffs off. He told me to just shut up and get into the cell. Three or four minutes later he came back into the cell and asked me if he could take the handcuffs off. I said, "Why do you want to take them off now?" He replied by saying, "Please let me take them off."

This was the first evidence of any courteous behavior that I had seen on the part of the police officer who had arrested me, and I allowed him to remove the handcuffs.

Another five minutes passed, and an officer came into the cell introducing himself as the lieutenant in charge of the district. He started to ask me some questions, when the arresting policeman came in with a couple of other policeman. At that point the lieutenant unlocked the cell and took me into his office where a Major Feliciano, who was in charge of the police delegation at the Pan-American Village, was using the telephone. When he finished talking, I told both officers exactly what I have recounted here. During the course of our conversation, the major said he hoped that I wouldn't look upon this as an example of Puerto Rican police work. I told him that I thought the officer involved was completely out of line and also assured him that this was the only negative incident with any Puerto Rican policeman that we had experienced since coming to the island. In fact, the Puerto Rican police, I told him, had been most cooperative and kind to us in escorting us around the island to practices and games.

About this time Colonel Don Miller, the executive secretary of the United States Olympic Committee, came to the police station. He was brought up to date on what had happened. I was asked if I wished to file charges against the policeman. I told them my only interest was getting this thing settled for just what it was: a minor argument between two people that should not have gone further.

The lieutenant asked me if I thought the policeman had hit me on purpose. I told him, "No, I don't think he did, but his accidentally striking me brought about the reflex action and subsequent push on my part." I also said that if they wished to pursue it, then I would have to do likewise. He agreed, as did the major, that it was something that should be settled without going any further and told this to both Colonel Miller and myself. With that we returned to the Pan-American Village.

It is important to note that the arrest and charges were not at any time supported by Puerto Rican or San Juan police agencies. Lacking such support, the police officer had to file charges as a civilian.

The policeman's subsequent story at the hearing to determine probable cause on Wednesday (July 11) morning involved a series of blatant lies;

his first lie was his statement that I had said, during the course of our argument in the gym, that all Puerto Rican policemen could go to hell.

Secondly, he said that I had hit him (while he had his head down writing in a notebook) by taking at least two powerful steps and swinging a powerful, roundhouse blow with my right arm and closed fist that struck the left side of his face. As I have said, my only contact with him was the reflexive push on his right cheek with my left hand.

Considering the difference in size between the policeman and myself, such a blow as he described would have caused at least as much damage as the blow delivered by Kermit Washington of the Los Angeles Lakers when he hit Rudy Tomjanovich of the Houston Rockets. As a result of that incident, Tomjanovich was not able to play for an entire season, and he required several operations.

The statements that I read from the district attorney's witnesses stated that I called the Brazilian women's team "niggers." Both of these statements are blatant lies. The policeman did not use either of these terms at the hearing. However, in the trial which followed on August 22, the policeman stated that I called the Brazilian women's team "whores" and called him a "nigger." Again, these are blatant lies.

Monday morning, July 9, I was asked by Colonel Miller if I would be willing to go to the police department where I had been taken when arrested to discuss the incident and work things out to an amicable solution for all concerned. I told him that I would, and accompanied him there along with the USOC attorney, Patrick Sullivan. We arrived shortly after noon for what was to be a 12:15 meeting. Fred Taylor and Mike Krzyzewski were also with us. After waiting forty-five minutes with nothing being done, we were asked to go to the municipal court building where we were told the meeting with all parties concerned would take place. After arriving there, Fred Taylor, Mike K. and I waited in the parking lot for over three hours without ever talking to anyone. Nothing happened and we returned to the Pan-American Village at approximately 5:00 P.M. Our game that night with Argentina was scheduled to begin at seven, which gave us just about an hour for the entire preparation for the game.

At 9 Tuesday (July 10) morning a press conference had been called by the U.S. Olympic Committee at the Hilton Hotel. This was the first time that I had been given an opportunity to tell my side of the incident and I was assisted in doing so by Fred Taylor and Mike K. Prior to that, I had been asked by USOC officials not to talk to the press and thought this was a real mistake in handling the situation, as did several members of the USOC Press Information Office. On Monday afternoon, I had insisted that a press conference be called or I would have to call it myself.

After the two-hour press conference, on Tuesday, we were asked to go to the court building once again to give our depositions to the district attorney's office. We were there as scheduled at 12:30 P.M. and waited for over an hour and a half until an English-speaking stenographer could be found to take our statements. The lady had a very difficult time since her English was not at all fluent. It was necessary for us to spell a great number of words for her. It took me almost two hours to give a fifteen-minute deposition in this manner. I returned to the Pan-American Village just in time to catch the team bus for our game with Cuba, which was to begin at 5:00 P.M. The entire preparation that we had for this game was Mike K. talking to Mike O'Koren and Mike Woodson, our team captains, on the telephone and having them relay the scouting information and what we wanted done to the rest of the team. Mike K. and Fred Taylor were not able to get to the arena for the game until three minutes before tip-off because of the language problems in giving their depositions. As was the case on Monday, none of the three of us had had a thing to eat all day long.

A hearing to determine probable cause in the case was set for 9:00 A.M. Wednesday. Mike K., Fred Taylor and I, accompanied by the USOC officials and our Puerto Rican lawyers, were at the court building shortly after 8:00 A.M. At this time, I was asked by my attorneys (who indicated they had been approached by the district attorney's office) if I would be willing to offer an apology stating that I in no way intended any actions to offend the people of Puerto Rico or the police department of Puerto Rico. I said I would be willing to do that as long as it did not include any implication that I was guilty or that I was apologizing to that specific policeman.

I was told by the Puerto Rican attorneys that the judge had stipulated that the policeman and I would each present our cases, supported by one witness apiece. As it turned out, the policeman was allowed to use two witnesses and I was permitted none. It was here that we learned that the charges that had been filed on my behalf against the policeman had been denied by the district attorney on the basis that the witnesses that I had, the Pan-American players, would be prejudiced on my behalf.

After hearing the testimony, the judge's decision was to uphold the charges against me for aggravated assault and a trial date of August 8 was set.

Immediately following the decision, our entire party assembled in a room adjacent to the courtroom. I asked the Puerto Rican attorneys if it were possible for me to be represented at the trial without actually being present. They did not know the answer and said they would investigate. I told them at that present time that, if this could legally be done, there was no way that I would attend the trial. I have maintained that position since that time. I was later told that the police officer and the district attorney were given a great reception by people in the lobby when they left the courtroom.

After first discussing with the attorneys what our next steps could and should be, I returned to the Pan-American Village to meet with Coach Taylor and Mike Krzyzewski.

Late in the afternoon, Pat Sullivan, Colonel Miller, and Bob Kane returned from meeting with the governor of Puerto Rico. We were told that the trial had been moved from Wednesday to Friday morning. I had said earlier in the week that I hoped this thing could be resolved before we left the island, and it was apparently this statement that led to the request that the trial be on Friday. However, both Coach Taylor and I immediately felt this was totally impossible because of the championship game being played that night between the United States and Puerto Rico and the tremendous strain on the members of our team who would have to spend the entire day in court.

In discussing all that had taken place (including a broken jaw sustained by Kyle Macy in a disgraceful incident during our Cuba game July 10) and the climate that now existed, both of them were of the opinion that we should withdraw the basketball team from further competition in the Games. After talking this over, we went to the team and explained to them the problems that we thought could be encountered if we remained. Our final decision to stay was reached because of all the time and effort the players had put into this and the tremendous, and actually increasing, desire they had to take the gold medal back to the United States.

On Thursday, we played Brazil in a game that started at one o'clock in the afternoon. Late that afternoon, Clarence Doninger, a close friend of mine and an Indianapolis attorney, arrived and was picked up by my wife at the airport. We discussed the entire situation with Mr. Doninger, and he immediately agreed with us that holding the trial on Friday was out of the question and totally unfair to our basketball team. His first order of priority was, therefore, to get it postponed.

The trial was set for 9:00 A.M. Friday in the municipal court building. Along with our attorney, Clarence Doninger, USOC officials, Coach Taylor, Mike K. and I arrived there shortly before 8:30. The previous night I had been told for the third time that an official approach had been made to my Puerto Rican attorneys about making an apology that would be acceptable to all concerned. I again agreed, stating that I was not guilty of the charges and, therefore, would not include that policeman involved in the apology. This was understood by all parties. The policeman refused to accept this, however, stating that I was no longer the issue but that the lack of support given him by the police administration was.

At no time that morning, July 13, nor before or after that did I ever make a commitment to anyone or indicate to anyone that I would return to Puerto Rico if the trial were postponed.

At one point I was told by Sabastian Carlo, former district attorney in Puerto Rico, that the only way to handle this matter was to go home and not come back. Carlo told Coach Taylor the same thing on another occasion.

From the morning of Wednesday, July 11, my position has been absolutely unwavering in not returning as long as that was legally possible. In asking for the trial to be postponed, the most prominent reason by my Puerto Rican attorney was the game that night. In talking about this, he loudly and emphatically said before the court with his hand in the air, "And it is a game that Puerto Rico will win." I told him afterwards that he wasn't any more right about that than he had been about anything else during the week.

At about 6:00 P.M. we were called and told that the game had been postponed from 9 until 9:30. The atmosphere at the game was the most emotionally charged of any athletic contest in which I have ever been a participant or a spectator.

In the 1976 Olympics in Montreal, Puerto Rico had lost to the United States by one point at the end of the game after leading most of the game. This was brought up many times in the two weeks leading up to our game with the Puerto Rican team in San Juan. The people there felt this was their greatest opportunity to defeat the United States. It was repeatedly called in print and elsewhere the most important single athletic event in the history of the island.

Prior to our game, the American Women's team played Cuba at 7:00 P.M. for the women's gold medal. The crowd en masse rooted for the Cubans to win, which they did. The arena had a capacity of ninety-five hundred.

An estimation of the actual crowd for our game went all the way to fifteen thousand. There was not an aisle or a doorway that was not completely blocked. The court was ringed five and six deep with spectators sitting on the floor. The Puerto Rican team came out on to the court after our team was already there and unfurled a gigantic Puerto Rican flag to the playing of the Puerto Rican national anthem. It is interesting to note that the American national anthem was not played until our players were presented with their gold medals after the game.

Just prior to the game's conclusion, I walked down the court and shook hands with the Puerto Rican coach and returned to our bench.

I just ask you for a moment to try to put yourself in my position at this point. I had been lied about and roundly criticized in both the Puerto Rican and America press. I, at first, just sat on the bench after congratulating all of our players. However, they soon came to me and a couple of them put me up on their shoulders where I shook my fist at the crowd, which was booing loudly and with a raised index finger, I indicated that, in spite of everything, we had taken all that could be thrown at us and we were truly Number One in the men's part of the Pan-American Games.

An impromptu press conference followed behind the bleachers while we were waiting to go back on the court for the awards ceremonies. I made some comments then that truly reflected my feelings at the time relative to how this whole episode had been handled. What I said I meant with some degree of humor, but for the most part it was not accepted this way.

I in no way intended for any remarks I made to reflect on Puerto Rico or the people of Puerto Rico. I was directing my remarks exclusively to those who had been involved with and had handled the situation as it was conducted in the courts of Puerto Rico.

Our team went back on the floor and while the awards were being presented to the Puerto Rican players I walked over and congratulated each one of them for not only the way they had played against us but the way they had played throughout the tournament. After the awards were presented to our players, the American national anthem was played and was accompanied by a great deal of jeering and booing.

Once again, following the on-court ceremonies, I answered questions for the press in front of our locker room. I mentioned how hard and well the Puerto Rican team played in the game. (Mr. Doninger was standing beside me.) I also said, when asked, that I thought Brazil was the next best team to the United States in the tournament. This apparently infuriated some of the Puerto Rican people associated with the basketball team, including an attorney named Marchand who later made several remarks about what a terrible person I am.

This ended for all of us what was a fifty-seven-day trip to the gold medal.

I have never been affiliated with, nor do I expect to be in the future, a group of players more deserving of being called champions than those members of the men's basketball team who represented the United States in the 1979 Pan-American Games.

Here are some points I particularly want to emphasize.

• I could attempt to fight through the Puerto Rican judicial system, but I have absolutely no experience with this system other than in the one case where charges were brought against me. I can only base my conclusion on the events surrounding this.

• From July 8 through July 13, I tried or agreed on four different occasions to reach a satisfactory conciliation through amicable means. I was rejected each time.

• An article appeared that is among the information you have been given on an incident involving a member of the Puerto Rican Yachting Team.

• The general runaround we were given throughout the entire week was an indication to all of us that no one really cared what our side of the story was. My charges against the policeman were not accepted by the district attorney's office. I was later told that the case could have been handled in such a way that it would have been impossible for my charges to be rejected by the court. At the probable cause hearing where I was to have one witness and the policeman one witness, it actually ended up that he had two witnesses and I had none as I have previously stated.

• Coach Taylor, Mike K. and myself, the three people who went through every single aspect of each event, concluded that there was absolutely no way that I had a chance with this case in court.

• It was clear to us that the only chance I would have would be to fight the inevitable conclusion of the case through the process of extradition which is what I have chosen to do.

• Also, as I stated earlier, several things that I have said have been interpreted to indicate a feeling of resentment toward Puerto Rico in general. This is absolutely not true, and I apologize for any such reflection or interpretation that could have been drawn from any remarks that I have made. Everything that I said as I have already stated was directed solely toward this specific incident and those people involved with it.

On the flight from San Juan to Miami on July 14, I told Clarence Doninger that not only was it impossible for this case to be won but that I would be given the maximum sentence, whatever that was. When that happened, I said I was not surprised, and I wasn't.

Col. Don Miller, executive secretary of the United States Olympic Committee; Bob Kane, USOC attorney, all worked extremely hard and put in long hours and labored with great concern in my behalf during the situation in Puerto Rico. I am extremely grateful for their efforts.

I also want to extend deep appreciation to Clarence Doninger and Stephen Ferguson who have brought the full strength of their skills and experience as attorneys to this case. Their help and counsel has been extremely beneficial to me.

APPENDIX B
Bobby Knight's Career Coaching Record

Army

Year	Overall	Pct.	Post-Season
1965–66	18-8	.692	NIT—4th
1966–67	13-8	.619	
1967–68	20-5	.800	NIT
1968–69	18-10	.643	NIT—4th
1969–70	22-6	.786	NIT—3rd
1970–71	11-13	.458	
ARMY TOTALS	102–50	.671	

Indiana

Year	Overall	Pct.	Big Ten	Pct.	Big Ten Finish	Post-Season
1971–72	17-8	.630	9-5	.643	Third	NIT
1972–73	22-6	.786	11-3	.786	First	NCAA—3rd
1973–74	23-5	.822	12-2	.857	First	CCA—1st
1974–75	31-1	.969	18-0	1.000	First	NCAA
1975–76	32-0	1.000	18-0	1.000	First	NCAA—1st
1976–77	16-11	.593	11-7	.611	Fourth	
1977–78	21-8	.724	12-6	.722	Second	NCAA
1978–79	22-12	.647	10-8	.556	Fifth	NIT—1st
1979–80	21-8	.724	13-5	.722	First	NCAA

1980–81	26-9	.743	14-4	.788	First	NCAA—1st
1981–82	19-10	.655	12-6	.677	Second	NCAA
1982–83	24-6	.800	13-5	.722	First	NCAA
1983–84	22-9	.710	13-5	.722	Third	NCAA
1984–85	19-14	.576	7-11	.389	Seventh	NIT—2nd
1985–86	21-8	.724	13-5	.722	Second	NCAA
1986–87	30-4	.882	15-3	.833	First	NCAA—1st
1987–88	19-10	.655	11-7	.611	Fifth	NCAA
1988–89	27-8	.771	15-3	.833	First	NCAA
1989–90	18-11	.621	8-10	.444	Seventh	NCAA
1990–91	29-5	.853	15-3	.833	First	NCAA
1991–92	27-7	.794	14-4	.778	Second	NCAA—3rd
1992–93	31-4	.886	17-1	.944	First	NCAA
1993–94	21-9	.700	12-6	.667	Third	NCAA
1994–95	19-12	.613	11-7	.611	Third	NCAA
1995–96	19-12	.613	12-6	.667	Second	NCAA
1996–97	22-11	.667	9-9	.500	Fifth	NCAA
1997–98	20-12	.625	9-7	.563	Fifth	NCAA
1998–99	23-11	.676	9-7	.563	Third	NCAA
1999–2000	20-9	.690	10-6	.625	Fifth	NCAA
Indiana Totals	661-240	.734	353-151	.700		
TOTAL	763-290	.725				

All together now, Hoosiers fans! (Nick Judy photo, Indiana University Instructional Support Services)

ENDNOTES

Chapter 1
1. "Playboy Interview: Bobby Knight," *Playboy*, August 1984.
2. *Courier-Tribune*, March 30, 1971.
3. *Courier-Journal*, February 7, 1973, reprint of *Louisville Times* article.
4. *The Courier-Journal and Times Magazine*.
5. *Courier-Journal*, February 7, 1973, reprint of *Louisville Times* article.
6. Deford, Frank, "The Rabbit Hunter," *Sports Illustrated*, reprinted January 10, 1994.
7. *Playboy*, August 1984.
8. Putnam, Pat, "Just a Gentle Sort of Man," *Sports Illustrated*, February 1973.
9. Ibid.
10. *Playboy*, August 1984.
11. Ibid.
12. *Indiana Daily Student*, March 6, 1997.

Chapter 2
1. *Courier-Tribune*, March 28, 1971.
2. *Bloomington Daily Herald-Telephone*, March 30, 1971.
3. Knight column "Off the Bench," *The Paper*, December 1977.
4. *Courier-Tribune*.
5. *Basketball, According to Knight and Newell*, believed to be self-published.
6. Ibid.
7. *Los Angeles Times*, March 5, 1976.
8. *Courier-Journal*, December 15, 1978.
9. *Cincinnati Post*, December 8, 1979.
10. *Bloomington Herald-Telephone*, April 27, 1994, quoting a Knight speech to a charity.
11. Deford, Frank, "The Rabbit Hunter," *Sports Illustrated*, reprinted January 10, 1994.
12. *Indianapolis Star*, November 15, 1985.
13. *Indiana Daily Student*, October 23, 1998.

14. *Indianapolis News*, February 8, 1980.
15. SportsUniversity.com.
16. *Indiana Daily Student*, September 14, 2000.

Chapter 3
1. *Touchstone*, Spring 1987, published by IU's Division of Extended Studies.
2. *Basketball, According to Knight and Newell.*
3. Ibid.
4. Ibid.
5. *Touchstone*, Spring 1987.
6. *Cincinnati Enquirer*, November 6, 1994.
7. Huber, Robert, "Bobby Knight Needs a Hug," *Esquire*, January 2000.
8. *Indianapolis Star*, March 5, 2000.
9. Ibid.
10. Ibid.
11. Ibid.
12. *Indianapolis Star*, November 18, 1990.
13. Ibid.
14. *Louisville Courier-Journal*, December 5, 1980.
15. Huber, Robert, "Bobby Knight Needs a Hug," *Esquire*, January 2000.
16. Wojciechowski, Gene, "Knight Takes His Hoosiers Beyond Mere Will to Win," *Los Angeles Times*, January 14, 1992.
17. Ibid.
18. Knight column "Off the Bench," *The Paper*, November 30, 1977.
19. Ibid.
20. England, David A., "Athletics, Academics, and Ethics: An Interview with Bob Knight," *Phi Delta Kappan*, November 1982.
21. Axthelm, Pete, "Will They Barbecue General Patton?" *Newsweek*(presumably), December 29, 1975.
22. Putnam, Pat, "Just a Little Gentle Sort of Man," *Sports Illustrated*, February 1973.
23. *Playboy*, August 1984.
24. Ibid.
25. Ibid.
26. Deford, Frank, "The Rabbit Hunter," *Sports Illustrated*, reprinted January 10, 1994.
27. Schoenfeld, Bruce, "The Mouth That Roars," *Profiles*, March 1993.

28. Ibid.
29. "General Comments: The World According to Knight," *Indianapolis Monthly*, November 1994.
30. Falls, Joe, *Detroit News*, January 5, 1996.

Chapter 4
1. *Playboy*, August 1984.
2. CNNSI.com, May 15, 2000.
3. *Arizona Daily Star*, February 9, 1975. Reprint of *St. Louis Dispatch* story.
4. Koster, Rich, "No Compromise," *St. Louis Globe*(?), July 14, 1977.
5. Axthelm, Pete, "Will They Barbecue General Patton?" *Newsweek*(presumably), December 29, 1975.
6. *Louisville Courier-Journal*, November 2, 1985.
7. *Indiana Daily Student*, September 14, 2000.
8. Putnam, Pat, "Just a Gentle Sort of Man," *Sports Illustrated*, February 1973.
9. Newman, Bruce, "Growing up with Bob Knight," *Indiana Daily Student Weekend*, February 15, 1975.
10. *Playboy*, August 1984.
11. Ibid.
12. Koster, Rich, "No Compromise," *St. Louis Globe*(presumably), July 14, 1977.

Chapter 5
1. Interview with Bob Costas on NBC's *Now*, and reported by Associated Press, March 17, 1994.
2. *Detroit News*, January 16, 1994.
3. *Courier-Tribune*, March 30, 1971.
4. Ibid.
5. *Indianapolis Star*, January 20, 1975.
6. *Playboy*, August 1984.
7. *Basketball, According to Knight and Newell.*
8. *Bloomington Herald-Telephone*, April 27, 1994.
9. Koster, Rich, "No Compromise," *St. Louis Globe*(presumably), July 14, 1977.
10. *Sports Illustrated*, February 22, 1981.
11. *Indiana Daily Student*, May 15, 1991.
12. *Fort Worth Star-Telegram*, March 20, 1987.
13. Huber, Robert, "Bobby Knight Needs a Hug," *Esquire*, January 2000.

14. Deford, Frank, "The Rabbit Hunter," *Sports Illustrated*, reprinted January 10, 1994.

15. Falls, Joe, *Detroit News*, January 5, 1996.

16. *Indiana Daily Student*, September 14, 2000.

17. Knight column "Off the Bench," *The Paper*, November 30, 1977.

18. Axthelm, Pete, "Will They Barbecue General Patton?" *Newsweek*(presumably), December 29, 1975.

19. Newman, Bruce, "Growing up with Bob Knight," *Indiana Daily Student Weekend*, February 15, 1975.

Chapter 6

1.   *Washington Post*, September 9, 1979.

2.   *Touchstone*, Spring 1987.

3.   Koster, Rich, "No Compromise," *St. Louis Globe*(presumably), July 14, 1977.

4.   Interview with Bob Costas on NBC's *Now*, and reported by Associated Press, March 17, 1994.

5.   *Washington Post*, September 9, 1979.

6.   Koster, Rich, "No Compromise," *St. Louis Globe*(presumably), July 14, 1977.

7.   *Indiana Daily Student*, January 7, 1989.

8.   *Louisville Courier-Journal*, February 19, 1980.

9.   *Louisville Courier-Journal*, June 24, 1988.

10. *Indiana Daily Student*, November 20, 1981.

11. Ibid.

12. Reed, Billy, "Knight Sees No Need for Apologies, *Louisville Courier-Journal*, July 17, 1979.

13. *Bloomington Herald-Telephone*.

14. *Indianapolis Star*, July 18, 1979.

15. *Bloomington Herald-Telephone*, August 25, 1979.

16. *Playboy*, August 1984.

17. *Indianapolis Star*, January 20, 1975.

18. Reed, Billy, "Knight Sees No Need for Apologies," *Louisville Courier-Journal*, July 17, 1979.

19. Newman, Bruce, "Growing Up with Bob Knight," *Indiana Daily Student Weekend*, February 15, 1975.

20. Ibid.

21. *Playboy*, August 1984.

22. Ibid.

23. Ibid.
24. Ibid.
25. Deford, Frank, "The Rabbit Hunter," *Sports Illustrated*, reprinted January 10, 1994.
26. "Indiana Coach Bobby Knight Throws Tantrums, Kicks Chairs—and Wins Basketball Games," *People*, March 15, 1976.

Chapter 7
1. *Basketball, According to Knight and Newell.*
2. Koster, Rich, "No Compromise," *St. Louis Globe*(presumably), July 14, 1977.
3. *Basketball, According to Knight and Newell.*
4. *Cincinnati Post*, December 8, 1979.
5. *Cincinnati Enquirer*, November 6, 1994.
6. *Arizona Daily Star*, February 9, 1975. Reprint of *St. Louis Dispatch* story.
7. *Courier-Tribune*, March 30, 1971.
8. *Basketball, According to Knight and Newell.*
9. Ibid.
10. *Indiana Daily Student*, September 13, 2000.
11. Newman, Bruce, "Growing up with Bob Knight," *Indiana Daily Student Weekend*, February 15, 1975.
12. *Basketball, According to Knight and Newell.*
13. Ibid.
14. Ibid.
15. *Detroit News*, January 16, 1994.
16. Ibid.
17. *Courier-Journal*, February 7, 1973, reprint of *Louisville Times* article.
18. *Springfield (Ohio) Daily News*, March 31, 1976.
19. Interview with Bob Costas on NBC's *Now*, and reported by Associated Press, March 17, 1994.
20. Hammel, Bob, *Bloomington Herald-Telephone.*
21. *Inside Indiana*, January 14, 1995.
22. Deford, Frank, "The Rabbit Hunter," *Sports Illustrated*, reprinted January 10, 1994.
23. *Playboy*, August 1984.
24. Ibid.
25. Deford, Frank, "The Rabbit Hunter," *Sports Illustrated*, reprinted January 10, 1994.
26. *Basketball, According to Knight and Newell.*

27. "Indiana Coach Bobby Knight Throws Tantrums, Kicks Chairs—and Wins Basketball Games," *People*, March 15, 1976.

28. *Indiana Daily Student*, September 13, 2000.

Chapter 8

1. *Washington Post*, September 9, 1979.

2. *Time*, April 13, 1987.

3. Huber, Robert, "Bobby Knight Needs a Hug," *Esquire*, January 2000.

4. Lidz, Franz, and Christian Stone, "Another Dark Knight," *Sports Illustrated*, June 26, 1995.

5. Koster, Rich, "No Compromise," *St. Louis Globe*(presumably), July 14, 1977.

6. *Washington Post*, September 9, 1979.

7. Deford, Frank, "The Rabbit Hunter," *Sports Illustrated*, reprinted January 10, 1994.

8. Ibid.

9. Hammel, Bob, and Larry Crewell, *The Champs, '81*. Bloomington, Indiana: The *Herald-Telephone* and Indiana University Press, 1981.

10. Ibid.

11. *Detroit News*, January 16, 1994.

12. *Arizona Daily Star*, February 9, 1975. Reprint of *St. Louis Dispatch* story.

13. Associated Press story as it appeared in *South Bend Tribune*, March 9, 1975.

14. Ibid.

15. Ibid.

16. Koster, Rich, "No Compromise," *St. Louis Globe*(presumably), July 14, 1977.

17. *Indianapolis Star*, November 18, 1990.

18. Associated Press, November 25, 1987.

19. Feinstein, John, *The Sporting News*, February 16, 1987.

20. *Bloomington Herald-Telephone*, February 25, 1985.

21. *Bloomington Herald-Telephone*, October 18, 1985, at a Union Board lecture.

22. *New York Times*, February 23, 1975.

23. Deford, Frank, "The Rabbit Hunter," *Sports Illustrated*, reprinted January 10, 1994.

24. Ibid.

25. Ibid.

26. Ibid.

27. Goodman, Mark, publication unknown.

28. *Indiana Daily Student*, September 14, 2000.

29. Ibid.

30. Looney, Douglas S., "He's IU's Knight Errant," publication and date unknown.
31. Deford, Frank, "The Rabbit Hunter," *Sports Illustrated*, reprinted January 10, 1994.
32. Hewitt, Brian, "Sport Interview: Bobby Knight," *Sport Magazine*, February 1982.
33. "General Comments: The World According to Knight," *Indianapolis Monthly*, November 1994 (from *Bob Knight: His Own Man*, by Joan Mellon).
34. Ibid.
35. *Louisville Courier-Journal*, date unknown.
36. *Los Angeles Times*, March 5, 1976.
37. *Playboy*, August 1984.
38. Deford, Frank, "The Rabbit Hunter," *Sports Illustrated*, reprinted January 10, 1994.
39. *Herald-Tribune*, May 15, 2000.
40. Deford, Frank, "The Rabbit Hunter," *Sports Illustrated*, reprinted January 10, 1994.

Chapter 9

1. Falls, Joe, *Detroit News*, January 5, 1996.
2. *Detroit News*, January 16, 1994.
3. England, David A., "Athletics, Academics, and Ethics: An Interview with Bob Knight," *Phi Delta Kappan*, November 1982.
4. *Playboy*, August 1984.
5. Ibid.
6. *Louisville Courier-Journal*, November 2, 1985.
7. *Cincinnati Post*, December 8, 1979.
8. *Indianapolis Star*, March 5, 1989.
9. *Playboy*, August 1984.
10. *Bloomington Herald-Telephone*, October 18, 1985.
11. *Playboy*, August 1984.
12. *Louisville Courier-Journal*, June 24, 1988.
13. Deford, Frank, "The Rabbit Hunter," *Sports Illustrated*, reprinted January 10, 1994.
14. *Fort Worth Star-Telegram*, March 20, 1987.
15. *New York Times*, February 23, 1975.
16. Goodman, Mark, publication unknown.
17. *Los Angeles Times*, March 5, 1976.
18. *Playboy*, August 1984.
19. England, David A., "Athletics, Academics, and Ethics: An Interview with Bob Knight," *Phi Delta Kappan*, November 1982.
20. *Bloomington Herald-Telephone*, October 18, 1985.

21. *Indiana Daily Student*, September 13, 2000.

22. Newman, Bruce, "Growing Up with Bob Knight," *Indiana Daily Student Weekend*, February 15, 1975.

23. Associated Press story as it appeared in *South Bend Tribune*, March 9, 1975.

24. *Saint Petersburg Times* article, which ran in *Bloomington Herald-Telephone*, May 1, 2000.

25. SportsUniversity.com.

26. England, David A., "Athletics, Academics, and Ethics: An Interview with Bob Knight," *Phi Delta Kappan*, November 1982.

27. *Cincinnati Enquirer*, November 6, 1994.

28. Hewitt, Brian, "Sport Interview: Bobby Knight," *Sport Magazine*, February 1982.

29. *Playboy*, August 1984.

30. *Louisville Courier-Journal*, June 24, 1988.

31. *Louisville Courier-Journal*, November 2, 1985.

32. "General Comments: The World According to Knight," *Indianapolis Monthly*, November 1994 (originally from *Time* magazine).

33. Looney, Douglas S., "He's IU's Knight Errant," publication and date unknown.

34. *Indianapolis Star*, January 20, 1975.

35. *Cincinnati Post*, December 8, 1979.

36. Koster, Rich, "No Compromise," *St. Louis Globe*(presumably), July 14, 1977.

37. Putnam, Pat, "Just a Little Gentle Sort of Man," *Sports Illustrated*, February 1973.

38. Koster, Rich, "No Compromise," *St. Louis Globe*(presumably), July 14, 1977.

(Indiana University Photographic Services)